AMMA SIDRA'S
AUTHENTIC
PAKISTANI
CUISINE

A TRUE TASTE OF PAKISTAN

Sheddy Hussain

Matador
Unit E2 Airfield Business Park,
Harrison Road, Market Harborough,
Leicestershire. LE16 7UL
Tel: 0116 2792299
Email: books@troubador.co.uk
Web: www.troubador.co.uk/matador
Twitter: @matadorbooks

ISBN 978 1805141 990

British Library Cataloguing in Publication Data.
A catalogue record for this book is available from the British Library.

Printed and bound by CPI Group (UK) Ltd, Croydon, CR0 4YY
Typeset in 11pt Minion Pro by Troubador Publishing Ltd, Leicester, UK

Matador is an imprint of Troubador Publishing Ltd

FOREWORD

Home is indeed where the heart is, but for me, home is also where taste buds come to life. If there is something that I didn't appreciate enough growing up, it has to be my mother's natural ability to cook delicious Pakistani food. Growing up in the UK, I was surrounded by many different cultures, but there was one constant that always reverted me to my roots: my mother's home-made cooking. The aroma of spices, the sizzle of the frying pan, waking up on Eid mornings to the delightful smell of sweet seviyan, were like a warm embrace, reminding me of my heritage and the culinary delights that came with it.

The older I got, the more I realised just how incredible my mother's cooking skills were. Without measuring ingredients, my amma would create dishes which highlighted a masterpiece of flavours and textures representing Pakistani cuisine's richness and diversity. And so, I felt compelled to share her legacy with the world.

My mum, Amma Sidra, was actually the inspiration behind my YouTube channel, Sheddy's Kitchen. But, as she would agree with me, a good ol' book is way better than watching something on a device!

That's why I created *Amma Sidra's Authentic Pakistani Cuisine*, a cookbook that celebrates the richness and diversity of Pakistani cuisine and shares my mother's culinary expertise with the world.

Whilst my mother's cooking style was intuitive, without needing quantities or measurements, I sat with her for hours to capture the exact ingredients and steps needed to recreate each dish accurately. The result? A cookbook that is not only a treasure trove of my mum's culinary expertise but also a guidebook for anyone looking to explore the diverse and untethered world of Pakistani cuisine.

Whether you're making a meal for your family or guests, these recipes will create a sense of intimacy and belonging at your dinner table – regardless of where you are in the world. A homage to Amma Sidra.

So, are you ready? Let's get cooking!

CONTENTS

(V): Vegetarian recipes

DESSERTS

SAUCES AND SIDES

STARTERS

ALOO KI TIKKI (V)
(POTATO AND PEA PATTIES)

Serving size: 2–3
Preparation time: 20 minutes
Cook time: 10 minutes
Calories: 214kcals per serving

NB: This dish goes really well with our Coriander Chilli Chutney (see page 76).

Ingredients

- 400g boiled potato (peeled and washed)
- 1 onion (finely grated)
- 100g garden peas
- 10g fresh coriander (finely chopped)
- 5 mint leaves (finely chopped)
- 2 green chillies (finely chopped)
- ½ teaspoon dried coriander powder
- ½ teaspoon cooking salt
- ¼ teaspoon cumin powder (Jeera)
- 3 teaspoons gram flour
- 2 medium-sized eggs (beaten)
- Sunflower oil (for frying)

Directions

1. In a bowl, add boiled potatoes and mash. Then add the onion.
2. Gently squeeze the garden peas and then add to the bowl. To this add the coriander, mint leaves, and green chillies.
3. To the mixture, add the coriander powder, salt, cumin powder, and gram flour. Gently mix everything together with your hands.
4. Create palm-sized patties with the mixture.
5. Dip patties into beaten eggs and fry in sunflower oil on medium heat for 2½ minutes on each side.
6. Remove patties, serve, and enjoy.

NB: This dish goes really well with our Coriander Chilli Chutney (see page 76).

Serving size: 4–6
Preparation time: 1 hour and 20 minutes
Cook time: 15 minutes
Calories: 253kcals per serving

FISH PAKORA
(FISH BHAJI'S)

Ingredients

- 1kg fish (cod) marinated in lemon and salt
- 200g onion (chopped)
- Handful mint leaves (chopped)
- 2 green chillies (finely chopped)
- 25g fresh coriander (chopped)
- 2 teaspoons pomegranate seeds
- ½ teaspoon red chilli powder
- 1 teaspoon red chilli flakes
- 1 teaspoon coriander powder
- 1 teaspoon cooking salt
- ½ teaspoon Ajwain (carom bishop's weed) seeds
- 150g gram flour (besan)
- Water (for mixing)
- Sunflower oil (for frying)

Directions

1. Refrigerate the fish for an hour or overnight.
2. Rinse the fish and drain. Chop into small chunks.
3. Place a pan on high heat with oil and fry the fish. Cook on both sides until golden brown. Remove the fish and allow it to drain. When cool, flake the fish in a bowl, removing bones.
4. Add onion, mint leaves, green chillies, coriander, pomegranate seeds, red chilli powder, red chilli flakes, dried coriander powder, salt, and bishop's weed.
5. Then add gram flour and a dash of water.
6. Mix together with hands until ingredients stick together.
7. Roll this mixture into cylinders and flatten slightly and place in oil to fry on medium heat. Cook for 2½ minutes and turn midway so that they are brown on all sides.
8. Remove from oil and place onto a tray lined with tissue to remove excess oil.

CHANA CHAT (V)
(CHICKPEAS)

Serving size: 2–3
Preparation time: 20 minutes
Cook time: 0 minutes
Calories: 176kcals per serving

Ingredients

- 480g drained chickpeas
- 600g cubed potatoes (pre-boiled)
- 3 medium-sized tomatoes (chopped)
- 200g onion (chopped)
- 4 teaspoons plain yogurt
- 3 pinches of red chilli powder
- 1 green chilli (finely chopped)
- ½ teaspoon cooking salt
- 1 lemon (juiced)
- 1 teaspoon chana chaat seasoning mix
- 2 pinches cumin seeds
- Sweet Thai chilli sauce

Directions

1. Place the drained chickpeas in a bowl. Add the boiled potatoes, tomatoes, onions, and the yogurt. Then add the red chilli powder, finely chopped green chilli, cooking salt, lemon juice, and the chana chaat seasoning mix. Crush cumin seeds with your hands and add to the mix.

2. Use a wooden spoon to gently mix everything together.

3. Plate and top with the sweet Thai chilli sauce.

CHICKEN CHAPLI KEBAB

(FLAT CHICKEN KEBABS)

Serving size: 4–5
Preparation time: 20 minutes
Cook time: 10 minutes
Calories: 214kcals per serving

NB: This dish goes really well with our Coriander Chilli Chutney (see page 76).

Ingredients

- 750g minced chicken thigh
- 125g minced onion
- 50g green chilli
- 40g fresh coriander (roughly chopped)
- 1 teaspoon cooking salt
- 1 teaspoon coriander powder
- 100g grated potato
- ½ teaspoon cumin powder (Jeera)
- Sunflower oil (for frying)

Directions

1. Add the chicken mince to a bowl. Then add the onion, green chilli, fresh coriander, salt, coriander powder, potato, and cumin powder.
2. Mix thoroughly with your hands.
3. Lay out some cling film on a counter.
4. Saturate fingers with oil. Take some of the meat and place it on the cling film. Repeat, placing each 10cm apart.
5. Cover them with cling film and use a dish to flatten them.
6. Remove flattened meat from the cling film and place it in a pot of oil to fry.
7. Lower the heat and allow the kebabs to cook thoroughly, flipping until each side is golden brown.
8. Remove from oil, drain and serve.

VEGETABLE PAKORA (V)
(ONION BHAJI)

Serving size: 4–5
Preparation time: 20 minutes
Cook time: 10 minutes
Calories: 246kcals per serving

NB: This dish goes really well with our Coriander Chilli Chutney (see page 76).

Ingredients

- 300g onions (sliced)
- 400g potatoes (sliced)
- 40g fresh coriander (chopped)
- 1 green chilli (chopped)
- 2 teaspoons red chilli powder
- 2 teaspoons coriander powder
- 1½ teaspoons cooking salt
- 350g gram flour
- 320ml tap water
- Sunflower oil (for frying)

Directions

1. In a mixing bowl, add onions, potatoes, coriander, green chillies, red chilli powder, coriander powder, cooking salt, and gram flour.
2. Slowly add water to the mixture, thoroughly mixing all ingredients.
3. Place the pot on high heat and add the sunflower oil.
4. Form pakoras using a tablespoon and add to the hot oil.
5. Fry until golden brown on each side.
6. Remove and drain pakoras on a kitchen towel and then serve.

TANDOORI ROAST CHICKEN

(MASALA ROAST CHICKEN)

Serving size: 8
Preparation time: 2 hours and 20 minutes
Cook time: 1 hour and 15 minutes
Calories: 234kcals per serving

NB: This dish goes really well with our Coriander Chilli Chutney (see page 76).

Ingredients

- 5 teaspoons lemon juice
- 3 teaspoons malt vinegar
- 1½ teaspoons red chilli powder
- 1 teaspoon cooking salt
- 1 teaspoon dried coriander powder
- 2 teaspoons dried fenugreek leaves (methi)
- 4 teaspoons natural plain yogurt
- 3 teaspoons tandoori masala powder
- 2 teaspoons Lahori charga spice mix (Shan or other)
- 8 chicken legs (scored)
- 4 teaspoons sunflower oil

Directions

1. To a bowl, add the lemon juice, vinegar, red chilli powder, cooking salt, dried coriander, dried fenugreek leaves, yogurt, tandoori masala powder, and Lahori charga. Mix well.
2. Coat chicken pieces with the mixture. Cover and allow to marinate for 2 hours in the refrigerator.
3. Preheat oven to 200°C/400°F/Gas mark 6. Spread sunflower oil on a baking tray. Add chicken to the tray and cover with foil.
4. Bake for 1 hour and 15 minutes. Flip halfway through and drain water if present.
5. Serve and enjoy.

MEAT SAMOSAS

(LAMB SAMOSAS)

Serving size: 8–10
Preparation time: 20 minutes
Cook time: 1 hour
Calories: 214kcals per serving

NB: This dish goes really well with our Coriander Chilli Chutney (see page 76).

Ingredients

Pastry

- 750g plain flour
- ½ teaspoon salt
- 3 teaspoons sunflower oil
- 500ml warm water

Filling

- 1kg minced lamb
- 475g onions (275g roughly chopped and 200g finely chopped)
- 500ml cold water
- 7 green chillies (chopped)
- 1½ teaspoons red chilli powder
- ½ teaspoon turmeric powder (Haldi)
- 1½ teaspoons of salt
- 200ml sunflower oil
- 750g parboiled potatoes (diced)
- 285g sweetcorn
- 450g garden peas (boil to soften and drain)
- 25g fresh coriander (chopped)
- 1 teaspoon coriander powder
- 1½ teaspoons cumin powder (Jeera)
- ½ teaspoon ground black pepper

Directions

1. To make the pastry, add the flour and salt to a bowl. Then add the sunflower oil and half of the water and mix. Add more water if needed. When the dough is formed, set aside.

2. Place meat in a large pan and place on heat. Add the roughly chopped onions and cold water. Also, add the green chillies, red chilli powder, turmeric powder, and salt and mix well. Cover and allow to cook for approximately 40 minutes. Check the pot occasionally to stir and ensure the meat isn't sticking to the bottom.

3. Add oil and mix. Cover and cook for 15 minutes. Mix occasionally until the liquid has reduced and the meat starts to brown. Then add the potatoes and sweetcorn. Add peas. Mix well and cook again for 5 minutes.

4. Add fresh coriander, coriander powder, cumin powder, and black pepper, as well as the finely chopped onions. Mix well to ensure all ingredients are evenly distributed.

5. Take some of the dough and make it into a ball. Press down on a floured surface and then roll to make a thin flat disk. Place down on a hot flat griddle and cook on each side. Score down the centre and then remove from heat. Repeat the process until all the dough is cooked.

6. Create a paste with plain flour and water. Use half of each cooked pastry to make a cone, using the paste to hold the shape. Add the meat mixture and close the top of the cone with the paste.

7. When the samosas have been made, fry them until golden brown.

8. Drain and serve.

MAINS

FISH MASALA
(FISH CURRY)

Serving size: 4–5
Preparation time: 2 hours and 20 minutes
Cook time: 20 minutes
Calories: 275kcals per serving

Ingredients

- 1½kg cod fish
- 1 lemon
- 300ml sunflower oil
- 600g onions (chopped)
- 2 teaspoons red chilli powder
- ½ teaspoon turmeric powder (Haldi)
- 1½ teaspoons salt, plus extra for marinating
- 2 medium tomatoes (chopped) or 400g tinned tomatoes
- 3 teaspoons garlic (crushed or paste)
- 2 teaspoons ginger paste
- 3 teaspoons dried coriander powder
- 1 teaspoon red chilli flakes
- 10 green chillies (chopped)
- 50g coriander (chopped)
- 2 teaspoons cumin powder (Jeera)

Directions

1. Cut fish into medium-sized chunks.
2. Marinate with lemon and salt for about 2 hours in the refrigerator.
3. Before cooking, rinse the marinade from the fish.
4. Heat the sunflower oil in a cooking pot. When hot, place the fish in the pot and fry on each side for about 2 minutes until slightly brown, and then remove the cooked fish from the oil.
5. Add the onions to the oil and cook until softened and brown.
6. Add red chilli powder, turmeric powder, and salt, and stir. If the consistency of ingredients begins to dry out, add a splash of water to soften onions and help them cook through. Then add chopped tomatoes and stir.
7. Add garlic, ginger, dried coriander powder, red chilli flakes, and chopped green chillies. Mix and cook for 2 minutes.
8. Lower flame. Place cooked fish pieces into the pot, cover, and stew for 2 minutes. Turn the fish on the other side and stew for 2–4 minutes. Add fresh chopped coriander and mix. Then add cumin powder and mix again. Serve and enjoy.

LAMB KARAHI

(LAMB CURRY)

Serving size: 4–5
Preparation time: 20 minutes
Cook time: 1 hour
Calories: 279kcals per serving

Ingredients

- 250ml sunflower oil
- 400g onions (chopped)
- 3 teaspoons crushed garlic
- 3 teaspoons crushed ginger
- 1kg lamb leg (chopped into small to medium chunks)
- 3 medium-sized tomatoes (chopped)
- 5 green chillies
- 1 teaspoon red chilli powder
- 1 teaspoon red chilli flakes
- ¼ teaspoon turmeric powder (Haldi)
- 1½ teaspoons cooking salt
- 500ml water
- 1½ teaspoons dried coriander powder
- 1 teaspoon cumin powder (Jeera)
- 50g fresh coriander (roughly chopped)

Directions

1. Place pot on high heat and add sunflower oil. When the oil is hot, add the chopped onions and cook until brown.
2. Remove half of the onions and set aside. To pot, with the remaining onions add crushed garlic and ginger. Mix well.
3. Add chopped pieces of lamb and stir. Then add chopped tomatoes and green chillies.
4. To the lamb, add red chilli powder, red chilli flakes, turmeric powder, salt, and mix well.
5. Add the water and bring to a boil and then lower the heat and cover with a lid. Cook until the meat is softened.
6. Then add dried coriander powder and stir. Cook so that most of the water has evaporated, and then add cumin powder, freshly chopped coriander, and the cooked onion that was previously set aside.
7. Mix and then remove from heat. Serve and enjoy.

CHANA DAL MASALA CURRY (V)

(SPLIT CHICKPEA LENTIL MASALA CURRY)

Serving size: 4–5
Preparation time: 20 minutes
Cook time: 20 minutes
Calories: 213kcals per serving

Ingredients

- 300ml sunflower oil
- 250g onions (chopped)
- 1 teaspoon red chilli powder
- ½ teaspoon turmeric powder (Haldi)
- 1½ teaspoons cooking salt
- 1 teaspoon ginger (finely chopped or crushed)
- 2 teaspoons crushed garlic
- 2 medium tomatoes (chopped)
- 2 green chillies (chopped)
- 2 teaspoons red chilli flakes
- 2 teaspoons dried coriander powder
- 300g chana dal (washed and soaked in water overnight)
- 1l boiled water
- 50g fresh coriander (chopped)
- 1 teaspoon cumin powder (Jeera)

Directions

1. Place pan on high heat. Add sunflower oil. When the oil is hot, add chopped onions. Cook until softened and browned.
2. Add spices: red chilli powder, turmeric powder, salt, ginger, and crushed garlic. Mix well. Add a splash of water if needed.
3. Then add chopped tomatoes and green chillies. Add red chilli flakes and coriander powder and mix.
4. Add chana dal and mix well.
5. After cooking for 5 minutes, add the boiled water. Mix and allow to cook until the dal has softened and most of the water has evaporated.
6. Add fresh coriander, dried cumin powder, and mix.
7. Lower the heat, cover, and allow to cook for 5 minutes.
8. Remove from heat and serve after a few minutes.

WHITE LOBIA MASALA CURRY (V)
(BLACK-EYED BEAN MASALA CURRY)

Serving size: 4–5
Preparation time: 20 minutes
Cook time: 20 minutes
Calories: 245kcals per serving

Ingredients

- 400g hard-boiled black-eyed beans (boil until partially cooked)
- 250ml sunflower oil
- 200g onions (chopped)
- 1 teaspoon red chilli powder
- ½ teaspoon turmeric powder
- 1 teaspoon cooking salt
- 2 teaspoons red chilli flakes
- 1 teaspoon crushed ginger
- 2 teaspoons crushed garlic
- 2 large tomatoes (chopped)
- 5 green chillies (slice lengthways)
- 1 teaspoon dried coriander powder
- 1l boiled water
- 50g fresh coriander (chopped)
- 1 teaspoon cumin powder (Jeera)

Directions

1. Place pan on high heat and add sunflower oil. When the oil is hot, add chopped onions. Cook until slightly brown.
2. Then add red chilli powder, turmeric powder, salt, and red chilli flakes. Mix well. Add a splash of water if the ingredients begin to stick to the pan.
3. To the mixture, add crushed ginger and garlic and mix.
4. Add chopped tomatoes, green chillies, and dried coriander powder. Stir all ingredients together.
5. Add drained black-eyed beans. After 13–14 minutes, add the boiled water.
6. Bring mixture to a boil and cover with a lid. Allow it to cook for about 15 minutes until the water has evaporated and the beans are thoroughly cooked and mushy.
7. Mix in freshly chopped coriander and cumin powder.
8. Allow the dish to cook for 1 minute, remove from heat, and serve.

MASALA ANDA CURRY (V)

(MASALA EGG CURRY)

Serving size: 4–5
Preparation time: 20 minutes
Cook time: 10 minutes
Calories: 235kcals per serving

Ingredients

- 250ml sunflower oil
- 350g onions (finely sliced)
- 2 green chillies (finely sliced)
- 1½ teaspoons red chilli powder
- ¼ teaspoon turmeric powder
- 1 teaspoon salt
- 1 teaspoon dried coriander powder
- 2 tomatoes (chopped)
- 50g fresh coriander (chopped)
- 6 medium-sized eggs (beaten)

Directions

1. Place pan on high heat and add sunflower oil. Then add onions. Cook until slightly brown.
2. Add green chillies, red chilli powder, turmeric powder, salt, and dried coriander powder. Mix and add a splash of water if the ingredients begin to stick to the pan.
3. Add chopped tomatoes. Mix in chopped coriander.
4. Turn the flame to low heat. Add beaten eggs and mix. Stir, breaking up eggs as they cook.
5. When eggs are cooked, remove from heat and serve.

CHICKEN KORMA
(CHICKEN COCONUT CURRY)

Serving size: 2–3
Preparation time: 1 hour and 20 minutes
Cook time: 20 minutes
Calories: 245kcals per serving

Ingredients

- 600g boneless chicken (chopped into large chunks)
- 75g whole-milk natural (plain) yogurt
- 2 teaspoons gram flour (besan)
- 1 teaspoon cooking salt
- 2 teaspoons ginger purée
- 2 teaspoons garlic purée
- 60g unsalted butter
- 2½cm cinnamon stick
- 1 large onion (finely sliced)
- 1 teaspoon ground turmeric
- 1 teaspoon chilli powder
- 3 teaspoons ground coriander
- 300ml warm water
- 6 teaspoons coconut flour
- 4 teaspoons sugar
- 50g raw unsalted cashew nuts
- 150ml double cream
- 1 teaspoon ground cardamom
- 1 teaspoon garam masala

Directions

1. Marinate chicken by adding yogurt, gram flour, cooking salt, ginger, and garlic purée. Mix well, cover, and marinate in the refrigerator for about 1 hour.
2. Place pan on medium heat. Add unsalted butter and add the cinnamon stick.
3. Add the onion and mix consistently for 5–6 minutes. Then add turmeric, chilli powder, and ground coriander.
4. Increase heat and add the marinated chicken. Add warm water and when the mixture has come to a boil, add coconut flour and sugar and stir thoroughly. Lower the heat, cover and simmer for 15 minutes.
5. Boil cashew nuts in water for 15 minutes, purée them, and then add cream. Add this puréed mix to the chicken.
6. Finally, add ground cardamom and garam masala and then mix.
7. Remove from heat and serve.

CHICKEN BIRYANI

(CHICKEN WITH MASALA RICE)

Serving size: 4–5
Preparation time: 20 minutes
Cook time: 30 minutes
Calories: 324kcals per serving

Ingredients

- 1kg Tilda basmati rice
- 400ml sunflower oil
- 2 medium onions (thinly sliced) and 350g onions (diced)
- 3 teaspoons red chilli powder
- 1 teaspoon turmeric powder (Haldi)
- 3 teaspoons cooking salt
- 3 teaspoons ginger paste
- 3 teaspoons garlic paste
- 350g small tomatoes (chopped)
- 2 teaspoons dried coriander powder
- 6 green chillies (sliced)
- 1 medium chicken (chopped)
- 1 lemon (sliced)
- Sweet peppers (sliced)
- 5 teaspoons plain yogurt
- 50g biryani powder
- 2 teaspoons cumin powder (Jeera)
- 25g fresh coriander (chopped)
- 2 mint sprigs (leaves chopped)
- 1½g saffron mixed with 2 tablespoons of water

Directions

1. Wash rice twice and then parboil. Drain the rice and set aside.
2. Place pan on high heat and add the oil. When the oil is hot, add sliced onions and cook until brown. After caramelising, remove onions from the oil and set aside.
3. Add the diced onions and cook until slightly browned. Then add red chilli powder, turmeric powder, and salt. Mix well. Add a dash of water to help soften the onions.
4. Add the ginger and garlic paste. Then add chopped tomatoes, mix, and allow tomatoes to cook until water is reduced.
5. Stir in coriander powder and green chillies.
6. Place chicken in the mixture, cover, and cook for 5 minutes, mixing periodically.
7. Then add lemon slices and sweet peppers. Also, add the plain yogurt and mix again.
8. Sprinkle biryani powder in the pot and mix well. Cook for a further 6 minutes.
9. Add cumin powder, fresh coriander, and chopped mint leaves.
10. Lower the heat and mix. Then remove from heat.
11. Place half of the chicken mixture in a pot and then add half of the rice to cover the chicken. Then pour in the rest of the chicken to cover the rice. Finally, cover with the remainder of the rice.
12. Add the browned onion on top of the rice and pour the saffron water over the surface of the rice.
13. Allow to steam for 10 minutes, remove from heat, and serve.

CHICKEN KARAHI

(CHICKEN CURRY)

Serving size: 4–5
Preparation time: 20 minutes
Cook time: 20 minutes
Calories: 245kcals per serving

Ingredients

- 250ml sunflower oil
- 250g onions (chopped)
- Medium-sized chicken (approx. 1kg cut into pieces)
- 2 teaspoons ginger purée
- 3 teaspoons garlic purée
- 400g tomatoes (chopped)
- 6 green chillies (chopped lengthways)
- 1 teaspoon red chilli powder
- ½ teaspoon turmeric powder (Haldi)
- 1½ teaspoons salt
- 1 teaspoon dried coriander powder
- ½ teaspoon black pepper
- 6 teaspoons plain yogurt
- ½ teaspoon crushed cumin seeds (Jeera)
- 50g coriander (chopped)

Directions

1. Place pan on medium to low heat. Add sunflower oil. When the oil is hot, add onions and cook until slightly brown. Then remove the onions and set aside.
2. Add the chicken. Add ginger and garlic purée and mix. Then add the tomatoes. Add three quarters of the green chillies. Leave the remainder to decorate the plate when serving. Add red chilli powder, turmeric powder, salt, dried coriander, and black pepper. Mix well. Cook for 13 minutes.
3. Add the plain yogurt and mix well. Add a splash of water when necessary to ensure that the chicken doesn't burn.
4. Then add crushed cumin seeds.
5. Reduce heat and cook until most of the liquid in the pot has evaporated. Then add the caramelised onions and the fresh coriander and mix.
6. Remove from heat, garnish with green chillies, and serve.

LAMB KOFTE ANDA CURRY

(LAMB MEATBALL AND EGG CURRY)

Serving size: 4–5
Preparation time: 20 minutes
Cook time: 1 hour
Calories: 267kcals per serving

NB: Boiled potatoes are optional.

Ingredients

Meatballs

- 1kg minced lamb
- 4 teaspoons blended onions
- 2 teaspoons blended green chillies
- 1 teaspoon dried coriander powder
- 1 teaspoon cumin powder (Jeera)
- ¾ teaspoon cooking salt
- 2 eggs

Other Ingredients

- 250ml sunflower oil
- 300g onions (chopped)
- 1 teaspoon red chilli powder
- ½ teaspoon turmeric powder (Haldi)
- 1 teaspoon cooking salt
- 200g tomatoes (chopped)
- 1 teaspoon crushed ginger
- 10 cloves garlic
- 1½ teaspoons dried coriander powder
- 1 teaspoon blended green chilli
- 4 teaspoons plain yogurt
- 1.6l water
- 50g fresh coriander (chopped)
- ½ teaspoon ground black pepper
- ½ teaspoon cumin powder (Jeera)
- 4 hard-boiled eggs (sliced)

Directions

1. Add minced lamb to a bowl. To that, add onions, green chillies, dried coriander powder, cooking salt, cumin powder, and eggs. Mix thoroughly with your hands. Oil hands and then make the meatballs.
2. In a pan, add oil. When the oil is hot, add onions and cook until brown. Mix occasionally.
3. When the onions have been browned, add the red chilli powder, turmeric powder, and salt. Mix well. Add a splash of water to help soften the onions.
4. Blend tomatoes with garlic cloves and ginger, and then add to the pot.
5. Add coriander powder and blended green chilli and mix well. Cook for approximately 5 minutes, stirring occasionally.
6. Then add the yogurt, mix, and allow to cook for 2 more minutes.
7. Add a splash of water (100ml), and then gently add the meatballs. Lower the flame. Cover and gently shake. Allow to cook for 2 more minutes. After this, shake again and allow to cook for another 3 minutes.
8. Remove the lid, and gently mix.
9. Increase heat to high flame and cook for a further 3 minutes. Add 1500ml of water. When the liquid comes to a boil, lower the heat and cover, and cook for 5 minutes.
10. Add fresh coriander, ground black pepper, and cumin powder. Stir and then remove from heat.
11. Serve with sliced boiled eggs.

ALOO CHANA CURRY
(CHICKPEA AND POTATO CURRY)

Serving size: 4–5
Preparation time: 20 minutes
Cook time: 20 minutes
Calories: 213kcals per serving

Ingredients

- 300ml sunflower oil
- 350g onions (chopped)
- 6 cloves garlic (finely chopped)
- 1¼ teaspoons red chilli powder
- ½ teaspoon turmeric powder (Haldi)
- 1½ teaspoons cooking salt
- 4 large tomatoes (roughly chopped)
- 700g potatoes (chopped)
- 800g tinned chickpeas
- 500ml water
- 1 teaspoon red chilli flakes
- 1½ teaspoons dried coriander powder
- 4 green chillies (chopped)
- 30g fresh coriander
- ½ teaspoon cumin seeds (Jeera)

Directions

1. Place saucepan on high heat. Add sunflower oil. When the oil is hot, add onions and cook until caramelised. Add garlic and stir.
2. When the onions are brown, add red chilli powder, turmeric powder, and salt, and then mix.
3. Then add tomatoes. Cook until mushy.
4. Add the potatoes and cook until they are tender. Then add the chickpeas, stir, and cook for another 3 minutes.
5. Add the water. Cook until it has reduced.
6. Stir in the red chilli flakes, coriander powder, green chillies, fresh coriander, and cumin seeds (crushed slightly with hands). Lower the heat, cover, and cook for 5 minutes.
7. Remove from heat and serve.

MUSHROOM CURRY (V)

Serving size: 4–5
Preparation time: 20 minutes
Cook time: 20 minutes
Calories: 234kcals per serving

Ingredients

- 300ml sunflower oil
- 400g onions (chopped)
- 1 teaspoon red chilli powder
- ½ teaspoon turmeric powder (Haldi)
- 1¼ teaspoons cooking salt
- 7 cloves of garlic (chopped)
- 5 medium tomatoes (roughly chopped)
- 2 teaspoons red chilli flakes
- 2 teaspoons dried coriander powder
- 3 green chillies sliced (lengthways)
- 1.3kg mushrooms (roughly chopped)
- 20g fresh coriander

Directions

1. Place saucepan on high heat. Add sunflower oil. When the oil is hot, add the onions. Stir and cook until brown.
2. Add red chilli powder, turmeric powder, salt, and a splash of water. Cook for about a minute.
3. Then add the garlic cloves and stir. To the mixture add the chopped tomatoes and cook until softened. After that, add chilli flakes, dried coriander powder, and green chillies, continue to stir to ensure that the mixture does not stick to the bottom of the pan. Add water if needed.
4. Add the mushrooms and mix thoroughly. Allow it to cook for a few minutes until the mushrooms have softened.
5. Then add the fresh coriander, mix, and then remove from heat. Serve and enjoy.

MASALA BHINDI CURRY (V)
(MASALA OKRA CURRY)

Serving size: 4–5
Preparation time: 20 minutes
Cook time: 20 minutes
Calories: 235kcals per serving

Ingredients

- 250ml sunflower oil
- 250g onions (chopped)
- 1 teaspoon red chilli powder
- ¾ teaspoon cooking salt
- ½ teaspoon turmeric powder
- 6 garlic cloves (thinly sliced)
- 4 medium-sized tomatoes (roughly chopped)
- 1 teaspoon dried coriander powder
- 4 green chillies (sliced lengthways)
- 500g okras or lady fingers
- 300ml water

Directions

1. Place pan on high heat. Add the oil. When the oil is hot, add the onions. Cook onions until slightly brown, stirring occasionally to prevent them from burning.
2. To the onions, add chilli powder, salt, turmeric powder, and sliced garlic cloves. Mix well. Add a splash of water to prevent the mixture from sticking to the pan.
3. Add the chopped tomatoes and coriander powder.
4. When the tomatoes become mushy, add the green chillies and okras.
5. Add water. Add the water to the pan and mix occasionally. Then lower the heat and allow the okras to steam for 5 minutes or until they have cooked thoroughly.
6. When the water has evaporated, remove from heat and serve.

KEEMA MATAR CURRY

(MINCED CHICKEN AND PEA CURRY)

Serving size: 4–5
Preparation time: 20 minutes
Cook time: 40 minutes
Calories: 268kcals per serving

Ingredients

- 300ml sunflower oil
- 300g onions (chopped)
- 1½ teaspoons red chilli powder
- ½ teaspoon turmeric powder (Haldi)
- 1½ teaspoons cooking salt
- 200g tinned tomatoes
- 3 teaspoons garlic (crushed)
- 2 teaspoons ginger (crushed)
- 3 medium-sized tomatoes (chopped)
- 2 teaspoons coriander powder
- 3 green chillies (chopped)
- 1½kg minced chicken (thighs)
- 3 pointy green peppers (halved)
- 400g peas
- 300ml water
- 25g fresh coriander (roughly chopped)
- 1 teaspoon cumin powder (Jeera)

Directions

1. Place pan on high heat. Add the sunflower oil. When the oil is hot, add the onions. Stir onions and cook until slightly brown.
2. Then add the red chilli powder, turmeric, and salt. Mix well. Add a splash of water if the ingredients begin to stick to the bottom of the pan.
3. Add the tinned tomatoes and cook until the liquid reduces.
4. Add crushed garlic and ginger to the mixture. Mix well.
5. Add the fresh tomatoes, coriander powder, and green chillies. Cook until the tomatoes are mushy.
6. Then add the minced chicken and mix thoroughly with the other ingredients. Add a splash of water to ensure that the mixture does not stick to the pan and burn.
7. After cooking for 15 minutes, add the green peppers and peas. Mix well and allow it to cook for 5 minutes. Remember to stir occasionally.
8. Add the water when the mixture starts to boil, add fresh coriander, cover, and lower the heat to medium.
9. Let it cook for 2 minutes. Add the cumin powder and mix well. Remove from the heat and serve.

MASOOR DAL CURRY (V)
(RED SPLIT LENTIL CURRY)

Serving size: 4–5
Preparation time: 20 minutes
Cook time: 20 minutes
Calories: 231kcals per serving

Ingredients

- 2l water
- 1½ teaspoons red chilli powder
- ½ teaspoon turmeric powder (Haldi)
- 1 teaspoon cooking salt
- 300g red split lentils
- 100g fresh coriander
- 200g salted butter (or 200ml sunflower oil)
- 6 cloves garlic (diced)
- 1 red onion (sliced and rinsed with salt water)
- Mint sauce

Directions

1. Add water to the saucepan and place on high heat. Add the red chilli powder, turmeric powder, and salt. Mix well to remove clumps. Cover until water begins to boil.
2. Remove the pot cover and add lentils. Mix well. Replace the lid and allow lentils to cook, mixing occasionally, until they are soft, and the mixture starts to thicken.
3. Add some fresh coriander and then remove the pan from heat.
4. Place another saucepan on medium heat. Add the butter and the diced garlic cloves. Allow the butter to melt and the garlic to become slightly brown.
5. Add butter and garlic mixture to the dal and mix well. Remove from heat and serve.
6. Mix onions with mint sauce with your hands and place on served dal.

GOBI ALOO CURRY (V)
(CAULIFLOWER AND POTATO CURRY)

Serving size: 4–5
Preparation time: 20 minutes
Cook time: 20 minutes
Calories: 234kcals per serving

Ingredients

- 275ml sunflower oil
- 250g onions (chopped)
- 1 teaspoon cooking salt
- 1 teaspoon red chilli powder
- ½ teaspoon turmeric powder (Haldi)
- 1 teaspoon crushed ginger
- 1 teaspoon crushed garlic
- 3 medium-sized green chillies (chopped)
- 3 medium tomatoes (chopped)
- 1 teaspoon dried coriander powder
- 350g potatoes (chopped)
- 1 medium-sized cauliflower (stems and head chopped into pieces)
- 25g fresh coriander

Directions

1. Place pan on high heat. Add the oil and then the onions when the oil is hot. Cook onions until they have softened and are slightly brown. Stir occasionally.
2. Add the salt, red chilli powder, turmeric powder, and mix well. Then add ginger and garlic and continue mixing. Cook for a few minutes, and then add the green chillies and the tomatoes.
3. Add the coriander powder and a splash of water if needed to prevent the mixture from sticking to the pot.
4. When the tomatoes are mushy, add the potatoes and stems of the cauliflower. Mix well.
5. Cook until the potatoes are half cooked, and then add the pieces of the cauliflower head. Continue to stir until the cauliflower is fully cooked.
6. Lower the heat and add the fresh coriander. Mix well, cover, and cook for a few more minutes.
7. Remove from heat and serve.

Serving size: 4–5
Preparation time: 20 minutes
Cook time: 1 hour
Calories: 321kcals per serving

LAMB CURRY
(TRADITIONAL HOMEMADE LAMB CURRY)

Ingredients

- 1kg lamb leg (chopped)
- 300g onions (chopped)
- 1½ teaspoons red chilli powder
- ½ teaspoon turmeric powder (Haldi)
- 1½ teaspoons cooking salt
- 1 teaspoon crushed ginger
- 1½ teaspoons crushed garlic
- 2 medium-sized tomatoes (chopped)
- 1 teaspoon crushed green chillies
- 2½l water
- 250ml sunflower oil
- 1½ teaspoons dried coriander powder
- 3 teaspoons plain yogurt
- 1 teaspoon cumin powder (Jeera)
- 25g fresh coriander (chopped)

Directions

1. Place lamb in pot and place on stove on high heat. Add the onions and cook for 6 minutes.
2. Add the red chilli powder, turmeric powder, cooking salt, ginger, garlic, tomatoes, and green chillies. Mix thoroughly before adding a litre of water.
3. Reduce to medium heat, cover, and allow to cook for 15 minutes, stirring occasionally.
4. Leave to simmer for 30 minutes and ensure that the meat is cooked and the liquid has reduced.
5. Add the oil and cook on high heat. Occasionally add water when needed to prevent the meat from sticking to the pan.
6. Add dried coriander powder, adding a splash of water when needed. Then add yogurt, mix, and then add remaining water.
7. Cook at high heat to reduce water. Then lower the heat and cook with the lid on for 3 more minutes.
8. Remove from heat, and then add the dried cumin powder and the fresh coriander. Mix well.
9. Serve and enjoy.

LAMB PILAU RICE

(TRADITIONAL BROWN RICE WITH LAMB)

Serving size: 4–5

Preparation time: 20 minutes

Cook time: 1 hour

Calories: 367kcals per serving

Ingredients

- 1kg lamb (neck, rib, and back)
- 2.5l water
- 2 teaspoons salt
- 1 green chilli (finely chopped)
- 1 small tomato (chopped)
- 375g onions (chopped)
- 25g whole mixed spices (whole garam masala)
- 1.2kg Laila basmati rice
- 400ml sunflower oil
- 300g tinned tomatoes (chopped)
- 1 teaspoon ginger
- 2 teaspoons garlic
- 1 teaspoon cooking salt
- 2 teaspoons garam masala powder
- ½ teaspoon ground black pepper
- 1 teaspoon cumin powder (Jeera)
- ½ teaspoon red chilli powder

Directions

1. Place a pan with the lamb on high heat, add the water. Then add salt, cover, and bring to a boil.
2. When the water is boiling, stir and loosely cover (there must be a slight gap to avoid boiling over) with the lid and continue to boil until the surface of the water is half covered with white foam impurities.
3. Skim the impurities from the liquid.
4. Then add the green chilli, chopped tomato, 100g onions, and the mixed garam masala.
5. Stir and place the lid partially on and allow to continue to boil until the meat comes away easily from the bone.
6. Rinse rice and then soak in lukewarm water for 45 minutes. Drain.
7. In a larger saucepan, place oil in to heat up. Then add the remainder of the onions, stir, and cook until softened and browned.
8. Then add the chopped tinned tomatoes, ginger, garlic, and salt. Mix. Boil until most of the liquid evaporates.
9. Add the meat from the broth mixture and brown.
10. Add the broth, garam masala powder, black pepper, cumin powder, and red chilli powder.
11. Allow it to come to a boil and cook for 3 minutes before adding the drained rice. Mix well.
12. Allow the rice to cook, and the water to reduce. When most of the water has evaporated, lower the heat. Cover and allow the rice to steam and cook thoroughly for approximately 20 minutes.
13. When rice is cooked, remove from the heat and allow it to rest for a few minutes before serving.

SURKH LOBIA/RAJMA CURRY (V)
(RED KIDNEY BEAN CURRY)

Serving size: 4–5
Preparation time: 20 minutes
Cook time: 20 minutes
Calories: 232kcals per serving

Ingredients

- 400ml sunflower oil
- 300g onions (chopped)
- 1½ teaspoons red chilli powder
- ½ teaspoon turmeric powder
- 1½ teaspoons cooking salt
- ½ teaspoon ginger (crushed)
- 1 teaspoon garlic (crushed)
- 3 medium-sized tomatoes (roughly chopped)
- 1½ teaspoons dried coriander powder
- 2 green chillies (chopped)
- 400g red kidney beans (boiled, reserve water)
- 1 teaspoon ground cumin (Jeera)
- Fresh coriander (for garnishing)

Directions

1. Place saucepan on high heat. Pour in sunflower oil. When the oil is hot, add the onions. Stir and cook onions until browned.
2. Add the red chilli powder, turmeric powder, and salt and mix well. Add a splash of water to ensure the ingredients do not stick to the pan.
3. Add garlic and ginger and mix. Stir well.
4. Then add tomatoes and chillies and mix well.
5. Sprinkle in coriander powder and mix, ensuring that the mixture does not stick to the pot. Cook until onions and tomatoes are mushy.
6. Add the red kidney beans and gently mix with the herbs and spices.
7. When the water evaporates, and the oil starts to come to the surface, pour in the water that the kidney beans were boiled in.
8. Cover and cook for approximately 10 minutes on low heat.
9. When the kidney beans are soft, remove the pot from the heat.
10. Mix in the cumin powder and garnish with fresh coriander.
11. Serve and enjoy.

PALAK (SAAG) ALOO CURRY (V)
(SPINACH AND POTATO CURRY)

Serving size: 4–5
Preparation time: 20 minutes
Cook time: 20 minutes
Calories: 212kcals per serving

Ingredients

- 300ml sunflower oil
- 300g onions (chopped)
- 1½ teaspoons of cooking salt
- 1 teaspoon red chilli powder
- 1 green chilli
- 1 teaspoon crushed chilli flakes
- ½ teaspoon turmeric powder
- 2 teaspoons crushed garlic
- 4 tomatoes (chopped)
- 1 teaspoon dried coriander powder
- 500g potatoes (chopped)
- 480g baby spinach (roughly chopped)
- 1 teaspoon dried fenugreek leaves (chopped)

Directions

1. Place pan on high heat. Add the sunflower oil. When the oil is hot, add the onions. Stir onions and cook until slightly brown.
2. Then add salt, red chilli powder, green chilli, crushed chilli flakes, and turmeric powder, and mix well. Add a splash of water if the ingredients begin to stick to the bottom of the pan.
3. After cooking for 2 minutes, add the crushed garlic. Mix in the tomatoes and allow them to cook until softened. Mix in the coriander powder.
4. Add the potatoes and a splash of water to allow them to soften.
5. Add the baby spinach to the pot and mix well. Add a splash of water if the ingredients begin to stick to the bottom of the pan.
6. Thoroughly cook potatoes and spinach, and then add the dried fenugreek leaves. Stir for a few minutes, and then remove the pot from heat.
7. Serve and enjoy.

CHICKEN CURRY

(TRADITIONAL HOMEMADE CHICKEN CURRY)

Serving size: 4–5
Preparation time: 20 minutes
Cook time: 20 minutes
Calories: 245kcals per serving

Ingredients

- 200ml sunflower oil
- 250g onions (chopped)
- 250g tinned tomatoes (chopped)
- 2 teaspoons red chilli powder
- 1½ teaspoons cooking salt
- ½ teaspoon turmeric powder (Haldi)
- 1 teaspoon grated ginger
- 2 teaspoons grated garlic
- 2 teaspoons dried coriander powder
- 1 medium-sized chicken (cut into chunks)
- 1.4l water
- 3 green chillies (chopped)
- ½ teaspoon ground cumin (Jeera)
- 40g fresh coriander (chopped)

Directions

1. In a large pot, add the sunflower oil. On high heat, allow the oil to get hot before adding the onions. Stir occasionally and cook onions until slightly browned.
2. Add chopped tomatoes, red chilli powder, salt, and turmeric, and mix well.
3. Cook until the liquid reduces. Add a splash of water to ensure that the ingredients do not stick to the bottom of the pot.
4. Add the grated ginger and garlic, adding splashes of water when needed.
5. Add dried coriander powder, adding water where necessary.
6. After cooking for a few minutes, add the chicken. Stir occasionally as the chicken cooks.
7. After 6 minutes or so of cooking, add the water. Cover and allow to cook for 10 minutes, allowing the water to reduce.
8. Add the green chillies and ground cumin and mix.
9. Lower the heat and allow to cook for a few more minutes.
10. Remove from heat, garnish with freshly chopped coriander, and serve.

DESSERTS

RASMALAI (V)

Serving size: 4–5
Preparation time: 10 minutes
Cook time: 10 minutes
Calories: 232kcals per serving

Ingredients

- 2l whole milk
- 600ml water
- 6 teaspoons sunflower oil
- 2 medium-sized eggs (beaten)
- 75g Rasmalai dessert mix (pistachio)
- 75g Rasmalai dessert mix (saffron)
- ¼ teaspoon salt
- 120g sugar

Directions

1. Place whole milk and water in a large pan and bring to a boil.
2. In a separate bowl, add sunflower oil and beaten medium-sized eggs. Mix gently. Add the Rasmalai mixes (pistachio and saffron) and mix gently until a thick paste is formed.
3. To the boiling milk mixture, add salt and sugar and mix well.
4. Roll Rasmalai mixture into small balls and add them to the milk mixture as quickly as possible. Allow to cook for 5 minutes, mixing occasionally. Cook for longer if a thicker consistency is desired.
5. Cool and then place in the refrigerator.
6. Serve when chilled and enjoy.

DOODH KI SEVIYAN (V)
(VERMICELLI PUDDING)

Serving size: 4–5
Preparation time: 5 minutes
Cook time: 1 hour and 20 minutes
Calories: 256kcals per serving

Ingredients

- 2l whole milk
- 500ml water
- ¼ teaspoon salt
- 100g sugar
- Cardamom seeds from 4 pods
- 100g vermicelli (broken into small pieces)
- 25g raisins
- Handful crushed almonds

Directions

1. Place milk and water into a pot and bring to a boil. Stir consistently.
2. Add salt, sugar, and cardamom seeds. Then add vermicelli. Cook for 3 minutes.
3. To the mixture, add raisins and cook until thickened (about 10 minutes).
4. Remove the pot from heat and allow the mixture to cool for an hour to thicken.
5. Add crushed almonds and serve.

GAJAR KA HALWA (V)

(CARROT HALWA PUDDING)

Serving size: 4–5
Preparation time: 15 minutes
Cook time: 45 minutes
Calories: 257kcals per serving

Ingredients

- 550ml full-fat milk
- 9 teaspoons milk powder
- 9 teaspoons whole-milk natural yogurt
- 250g butter
- 5 cardamom seeds
- 2½kg grated carrots
- 300g sugar
- ¼ teaspoon salt
- 15g coconut (chopped)
- 75g almonds (chopped into quarters)
- 25g raisins

Directions

1. In a pot, bring the milk to a boil, then add the natural yogurt. When the mixture begins to clump, remove it from the heat and drain using a sieve. Then add the milk powder to the clumps and mix, breaking the clumps into smaller pieces.
2. Place pan on high heat and add butter to melt. As the butter is melting, add the cardamom seeds. Then add the grated carrots and sugar and mix periodically for about 30 minutes. Add water if needed to prevent burning.
3. Add salt and mix. Then add half of the raisins and half of the almonds to the cooking mixture. Add the coconut.
4. Then remove from heat and add the previously prepared mixture of the milk, milk powder, and yogurt.
5. Garnish with the rest of the raisins and almonds, serve, and enjoy!

MEETHE CHAWAL/ZARDA (V)

(SWEET RICE DESSERT)

Serving size: 4–5
Preparation time: 1 hour and 20 minutes
Cook time: 30 minutes
Calories: 311 kcals per serving

Ingredients

- 1kg rice
- 7l water
- ½ lemon (juiced)
- 375g unsalted butter
- Seeds from 6 cardamom pods
- 800g granulated sugar
- ½ orange (juice and peel)
- 75g almond slices
- 40g raisins
- 25g coconut (sliced)
- ½ teaspoon salt
- 2 teaspoons kewra or rosewater
- 100g glazed cherries
- Food colouring

Directions

1. Wash rice twice with cold water. Then soak for 1 hour. Drain.
2. Boil 4l water and add the lemon juice. Then add the drained rice and gently stir. Cook until al dente. Remove the pot from heat, drain the rice, and rinse with cold water.
3. In a pan, add unsalted butter. When melted, add cardamom seeds.
4. Add 3l water and sugar. Mix and allow the sugar to dissolve.
5. Then add the orange peel, almonds, raisins, and coconut and stir.
6. Add salt and orange juice.
7. Place drained rice into the mixture and gently stir. Cook until most of the water has evaporated.
8. Add kewra and cherries.
9. Add food colouring to various sections of the mixture. Cover and allow to steam on low heat for 15 minutes.
10. Remove from heat and allow to cook for 10 minutes. Mix and then serve.

KHEER (V)
(RICE PUDDING)

Serving size: 4–5
Preparation time: 10 minutes
Cook time: 1 hour and 40 minutes
Calories: 224kcals per serving

Ingredients

- 2.5l water
- 300g pudding rice
- ¼ teaspoon cooking salt
- 2.3l whole milk
- Seeds from 5 cardamom pods
- 125g unsalted butter
- 200g sugar
- 25g raisins
- 50g coconut (chopped)
- 25g crushed almonds

Directions

1. Add water to a pan. Place on high heat.
2. When the water is boiling, add the rice and the salt. Mix occasionally until the water reduces and the rice is cooked.
3. Lower the heat, and then add the milk and cardamom seeds. Mix well and cook on high heat until the liquid has reduced again. Mix frequently.
4. Add the butter, sugar, raisins, and coconut. Allow the mixture to continue to boil, and the butter to melt.
5. Lower to medium heat and cook until the mixture has thickened, and the rice is mushy.
6. Remove from heat and let cool for 1 hour.
7. Sprinkle almonds on top and serve.

SWEET SEVIYAN (V)

(VERMICELLI)

Serving size: 4–5
Preparation time: 20 minutes
Cook time: 20 minutes
Calories: 245kcals per serving

Ingredients

- 4 green cardamom pods (seeds ground)
- 600ml water
- 100g granulated sugar
- 2 pinches salt
- 150g unsalted butter
- 250g roasted vermicelli
- 50g raisins

Directions

1. In a saucepan, place the cardamom seeds, water, sugar, and salt. Place on high heat until boiling. Remove from heat.
2. Break vermicelli into pieces.
3. Place another pan on low heat and add the butter. Allow the butter to melt and add the vermicelli.
4. Stir the vermicelli in the butter gently, ensuring that it is not sticking. Cook until brown.
5. Add the previously prepared liquid. Lower the heat, cover, and allow the vermicelli to cook thoroughly.
6. Remove from heat and scatter the raisins over the surface. Serve and enjoy!

PUMPKIN HALWA (V)

(PUMPKIN PUDDING)

Serving size: 4–5
Preparation time: 15 minutes
Cook time: 15 minutes
Calories: 256kcals per serving

Ingredients

- 2 medium-sized pumpkins (deseeded, peeled, and cubed)
- 400ml water
- 200g sugar
- 250g salted butter
- 4 green cardamom pods (Elaichi)
- Crushed almonds (to serve)

Directions

1. Place pumpkin in a large pan. Turn on the stove to high heat. Add water. Cook for about 12 minutes, until the water has evaporated, stirring to ensure that all the pumpkin is equally cooked.
2. When the pumpkin is soft, add the sugar and stir.
3. In another saucepan on low heat, add the butter and cardamom pods, and allow the butter to melt and cook for a few minutes.
4. Then add the butter mixture to the pumpkin mixture. Stir well and mix continuously.
5. Remove from heat, add crushed almonds as a garnish, and serve.

SAUCES AND SIDES

CORIANDER CHILLI CHUTNEY (V)

Serving size: 2–3
Preparation time: 20 minutes
Cook time: 0 minutes
Calories: 75kcals per serving

Ingredients

- 235g plain yogurt
- 3 green chillies (roughly chopped)
- 2 cloves garlic
- 80g coriander (chopped)
- Leaves of 3 mint sprigs
- ½ teaspoon cooking salt
- ½ teaspoon coriander powder

Directions

1. Add yogurt to the blender. Then add the green chillies, garlic, fresh coriander, mint leaves, salt, and coriander powder.
2. Blend.
3. Pour into dish and serve.

CHAPATI (ROTI) (V)

Serving size: 4–5
Preparation time: 20 minutes
Cook time: 5 minutes
Calories: 80kcals per serving

Ingredients

- 300g medium chapati flour
- 200ml water

Directions

1. Gradually add water to flour to form a dough. Knead it to soften the dough mixture.
2. Leave for 10 minutes to rest. Then add water to one's hand and knead the dough to soften it again. Let it rest for 5 more minutes.
3. Place some of the dough mixture in your hand, pat it into the flour, and create a ball.
4. Place the dough ball on a floured surface, press with your hands, and then roll with a rolling pin until the thickness of a 1p coin.
5. Preheat the hot plate. Place flattened dough on the hot plate and allow it to cook on one side, and then flip and cook on the other side. Continue to flip until fully cooked. Repeat until the dough is finished. Wrap chapatis in tea cloth to help them remain soft until ready to be served.

PARATHA (V)
(BUTTERED CHAPATI)

Serving size: 4–5
Preparation time: 20 minutes
Cook time: 5 minutes
Calories: 154kcals per serving

Ingredients

- 400g medium chapati flour
- Pinch of salt
- 250ml water
- 100g margarine

Directions

1. Add the flour to a bowl, add a pinch of salt, and mix.
2. Add water gradually whilst kneading the dough.
3. Leave the dough for 10 minutes to settle and then knead again to soften and leave for 5 more minutes.
4. Make dough into two balls, then flatten the balls into disks.
5. Put 15g margarine onto the centre of one disk and spread it (to cover disk). Place the other dough disk on top. The margarine should be sandwiched in between the disks.
6. Using a rolling pin, gently roll out the dough into a large circle (about the size of dinner plate).
7. Place on a hot plate and add 2.5g margarine to the top. After a few minutes, flip the paratha and add 2.5g margarine to the top. Leave to brown for a few more minutes and remove from the hot plate. Repeat the process for the rest of parathas.

NAAN BREAD (V)

Serving size: 10

Preparation time: overnight for dough to rise and 20 minutes (for cooking)

Cook time: 5 minutes

Calories: 189kcals per serving

Ingredients

- 750g self-raising flour
- ½ teaspoon cooking salt
- 2 teaspoons granulated sugar
- 1 medium-sized egg
- 5g yeast
- 500ml lukewarm water
- 200ml sunflower oil
- 4 teaspoons natural plain yogurt
- Handful of sesame seeds

Directions

1. Place the flour in a bowl and add the salt. Then add the sugar and egg and mix.

2. Add the yeast and mix. Slowly add the water and start mixing. Add water as needed to create a sticky dough. Cover and leave overnight for the dough to rise.

3. Oil your hands. Take some of the dough and roll it into a ball. Place it on a floured surface and roll it out.

4. Mix the yogurt with the oil.

5. Place rolled dough on a hot plate. When bubbles begin to form, remove from heat and spread the oil and yogurt mixture on top. Then place the dough in the oven to finish the cooking process, until the top is golden brown. Sprinkle on sesame seeds. Cover with a tea cloth.

6. Repeat the process until all the dough has been used.